CONTENTS

UNSOLVED MYSTERIES

For hundreds of years, people have been interested in and puzzled by mysterious places, creatures and events. Why do ships and planes vanish without trace when they cross the Bermuda Triangle? Are some houses really haunted by ghosts? Does the Abominable Snowman actually exist? What secrets does a black hole hold? These mysteries have baffled scientists, who have spent years trying to find the answers. But just how far can science go? Can it really explain the seemingly unexplainable? Or are there some mysteries which science simply cannot solve? Read on, and make your own mind up...

This book tells you about the mystery of black holes. It explains why **astronomers** think that black holes exist, what causes them, what they are like inside and the search to find black holes in space.

In billions of years time, the Universe could end as all the matter in it flows into a colossal, unseen black hole.

What is a black hole?

A black hole is a place in space where **gravity** is super-strong; so strong that nothing can escape from it – not even light, the fastest known thing in the Universe. This means that anything that falls into the hole never comes out.

Astronomers think that near to and inside black holes, events become very strange indeed. Time and space are warped, and the laws of physics that we learn at school no longer apply. Nobody could ever go into these mysterious places to investigate because they would never return.

In most great mysteries, such as UFOs, science comes second. It tries to explain the strange things that people claim to have experienced. In the case of black holes, however, things are the other way round. Scientists predicted that they should exist long before there was any real evidence that they really did. In fact, the very nature of a black hole means they cannot be seen to be believed!

So how did astronomers come to predict the existence of such mysterious things, and what can they do to prove that they really exist?

GRAVITY, LIGHT AND MOTION

To understand what **astronomers think** happens in black holes, we have to enter the world of **astrophysics** (the branch of physics that attempts to explain what happens in the Universe). To understand even the simplest astrophysics, we have to know about **gravity**: what it is, how it makes things move and how light travels.

All about gravity

Gravity is a **force** that attracts (pulls together) every body (an object which has mass) in the Universe towards every other body in the Universe. The size of the gravitational pull between two bodies depends on the mass of the two bodies and the distance between them. The bigger the masses, the bigger the force. The bigger the distance between them, the smaller the force. In fact, if the distance is doubled, the force is quartered. The size of the gravitational pull between bodies is very tiny unless one of the bodies is very massive, such as a planet.

This is called the Law of Universal Gravitation. It was first written down by the famous English scientist Sir Isaac Newton (1642–1727). It successfully explained how the gravitational pull between the Sun and planets made the planets **orbit** the Sun.

Sir Isaac Newton developed theories in mathematics and physics which scientists still use today.

You can think of a body as having a **gravitational field** around it. Any other object in the field experiences a pull from the body which pulls the object towards it.

The nature of light

Light travels in straight lines called rays. We see things because light rays from them enter our eyes, which detect the light. We see some objects, such as stars, because they make light. We see others, such as planets or this book, because light bounces off them. Light travels very fast indeed. In space, where there is a **vacuum**, its speed is 300,000 kilometres per second. Its speed reduces when it passes through substances, such as air and glass.

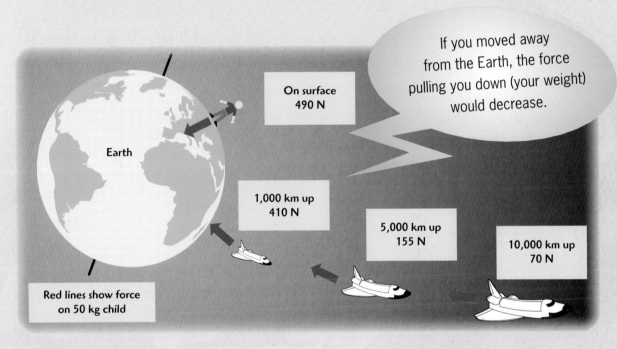

If you moved away from the Earth, the force pulling you down (your weight) would decrease.

On surface
490 N

Earth

1,000 km up
410 N

5,000 km up
155 N

10,000 km up
70 N

Red lines show force on 50 kg child

Mass and weight

Mass and weight are often confused. In physics, the mass of an object is the amount of matter in it. Mass is measured in kilograms (kg). Weight is the pull of gravity between an object and the planet or moon it is on. It is a force and is measured in newtons (N). The mass of an object is always the same, but its weight can change.

EARLY THEORIES

With black holes featuring in science-fiction movies, you might think of them as an invention of the 20th century. But ideas about strange objects, different to the stars and planets that astronomers of the time could see, were actually put forward hundreds of years ago.

Light and gravity

When Newton devised his Law of Universal Gravitation, he also suggested that light was subjected to the pull of **gravity**. On Earth, light always travels in a straight line (unless it hits an object). But light rays do get bent as they pass close to bodies that have very strong **gravitational fields**, such as very massive stars. This shows that the things we take for granted on Earth do not necessarily apply when super-strong gravity is at work.

Stars appear to change position when light from them passes close to another star on its way to Earth.

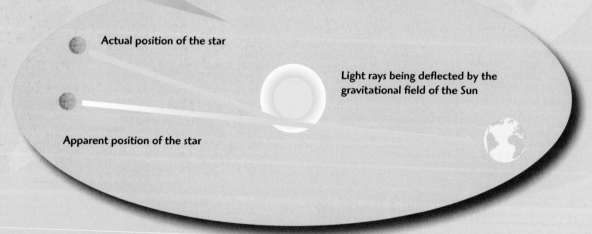

Actual position of the star

Light rays being deflected by the gravitational field of the Sun

Apparent position of the star

Dark stars

One of the first people to suggest that black holes could exist was the French mathematician and astronomer Pierre Laplace (1749–1827). He was an expert on celestial mechanics (how the planets and moons move around the Sun). In a book called *Exposition of the System of the World*, published in 1795, Laplace made an amazing prediction.

Laplace realized that if a star were massive enough, its escape velocity (see below) would be greater than the speed of light. So he calculated how big a star would have to be, if it was the same overall **density** as the Earth, to have an escape velocity equal to the speed of light. He calculated that the star would have to be 250 times the **diameter** of the Sun. So Laplace predicted that a star of this size would have such an enormous gravitational pull that light from it would never reach the outside world, and the star would therefore be invisible.

Space rockets must accelerate to a minimum of 28,000 km/h in order to stay in **orbit** around the Earth, but must travel faster to escape from the Earth.

Escape velocity

Imagine throwing a ball straight upwards. The Earth's gravity would gradually slow it down and make it fall back to you. But if you could throw the ball upwards fast enough, gravity would not be able to stop it escaping into space. The minimum speed needed for this to happen is called escape velocity. On Earth it is 40,000 kilometres per hour (km/h).

CHANGING THE RULES

There are vital differences between Laplace's idea of a 'dark' star and the modern idea of a black hole. Laplace did not know about two important discoveries of modern **astrophysics**. The first is that nothing can travel faster than light. This means that if light cannot escape from a massive star, nothing can. This effectively turns a 'dark' star into a hole, because anything that is pulled in by the star's **gravity** can never escape. The second difference is that Laplace used Newton's laws of gravity as the basis of his work. We now know that these laws do not work in and around black holes.

Albert Einstein aged 42. His Special Theory of Relativity was published when he was just 26.

Everything is relative

The person responsible for predicting these theoretical differences was perhaps the most famous scientist of all time, Albert Einstein (1879–1955). In his revolutionary General Theory of Relativity, Einstein put forward a new theory about the size of gravitational **forces**. Newton's and Einstein's theories give almost exactly the same answer on Earth, where the **gravitational field** is quite weak, but they differ enormously for super-strong gravity. Einstein had shown that Newton's laws were useless for predicting what would happen in black holes.

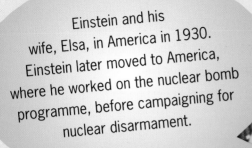

Einstein and his wife, Elsa, in America in 1930. Einstein later moved to America, where he worked on the nuclear bomb programme, before campaigning for nuclear disarmament.

More relativity

Einstein also made other predictions in his General Theory of Relativity. These were predictions that it is hard to understand when you are used to the way things behave on Earth, with its low gravity. For a start, Einstein said that in super-strong gravitational fields, time passes more slowly than it does outside the field. And as gravity becomes **infinitely** strong, time slows to a stop. He also said that all the laws of **geometry** would no longer be true because three-dimensional space would be distorted. So for example, the area of a square would no longer be equal to its length multiplied by its width.

Einstein's other great theory, the Special Theory of Relativity, predicted that the passing of time and the measurement of distance change as you move faster and faster. But the effects only become noticeable as you approach the speed of light. This would also have consequences for black holes, since objects which fall into black holes would be accelerated to the speed of light.

A THEORETICAL BLACK HOLE

Armed with Einstein's theories, the German **astronomer**
Karl Schwarzschild (1873–1916) developed the idea of
the black hole as we know it today. He did not call it a
black hole at the time – the term was coined in the late
1960s by the American physicist John Wheeler.

Karl Schwarzschild,
who published his first
scientific paper at the age of just 16,
and became a professor
of astronomy at 28.

Gravitational radius

Laplace used Newton's laws to calculate
the size of a body which would stop light
escaping. Schwarzschild calculated at what
distance from the centre of a body the escape
velocity would be the speed of light, but he used Einstein's
relativity theory. Remember that the **force** of **gravity** between two
objects gets larger and larger as the objects get closer together.
At a certain distance from a body, the gravity becomes so large
that the escape velocity becomes greater than the speed of light.

Schwarzschild calculated that this distance, in kilometres, would be about three times the mass of the body in solar units (the number of times more massive the body is than the Sun). This distance is known as the **gravitational radius** or Schwarzschild **radius**.

It is possible to calculate the gravitational radius of any object (or body) in space. For normal bodies, such as planets and stars, the gravitational radius is much smaller than the body. For example, it is just one centimetre for the Earth, for which the total radius is 6,378 kilometres, and it is three kilometres for the Sun, which has a radius of 700,000 kilometres.

Schwarzschild's theory was that a black hole was formed if the gravitational radius of a body was larger than its actual radius. This would require a body to be squeezed into an extremely tiny space. For example, the Earth would have to be squashed to the size of a pea to become a black hole.

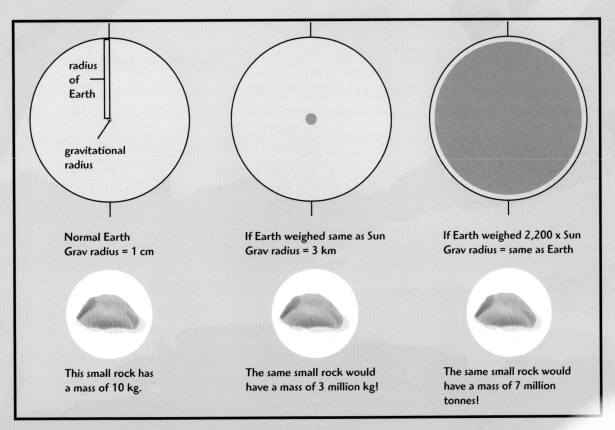

radius
of
Earth

gravitational
radius

Normal Earth
Grav radius = 1 cm

If Earth weighed same as Sun
Grav radius = 3 km

If Earth weighed 2,200 x Sun
Grav radius = same as Earth

This small rock has
a mass of 10 kg.

The same small rock would
have a mass of 3 million kg!

The same small rock would
have a mass of 7 million
tonnes!

WHERE DO BLACK HOLES COME FROM?

Karl Schwarzschild predicted that black holes would be formed when a massive star stopped shining and collapsed in on itself because of **gravity**. The gravity would be so large that the material would become more and more dense, making the gravity still stronger. Gravity would eventually become so large that the star would keep collapsing past its **gravitational radius**. Once past this point, there would be nothing to stop the star collapsing until nothing was left except a **gravitational field**! In 1939, American **astrophysicists** Robert Oppenheimer and Hartland Snyder used mathematics to show that this collapse would happen.

The Orion nebula, a huge cloud of gas and dust lit by the light of nearby stars.

The life of stars

Before looking at how a star collapses to become a black hole, let's look at the rest of its life. Stars are formed inside vast clouds of gas and dust called **nebulae**. Over billions of years, gravity causes the gas and dust to drift together to form clumps called protostars. Each protostar shrinks until its centre becomes so dense that nuclear reactions start inside and it starts to shine.

Stars come in different sizes. Our Sun is a pretty average star which glows yellow. Larger stars glow blue or white because they are hotter, but they don't shine for as long. Smaller stars glow orange or red. They are cooler and last longer.

After thousands of millions of years, the nuclear reactions in the Sun will stop. Gravity will then squeeze the core, creating heat which will make the outer layers swell, swallowing up the Earth. The outer layers will drift into space leaving a planet-sized body called a white dwarf.

Supernovas and neutron stars

Stars more than 10 times more massive than the Sun end their lives in a different way. The core squeezes itself so much that there is a huge explosion called a supernova. Sometimes the heavy core turns into something called a neutron star which is just a few kilometres across. The material of a neutron star is very dense indeed – a piece the size of a grain of sand weighs a million tonnes! If the core is twice as heavy as the Sun, it keeps collapsing to become a black hole.

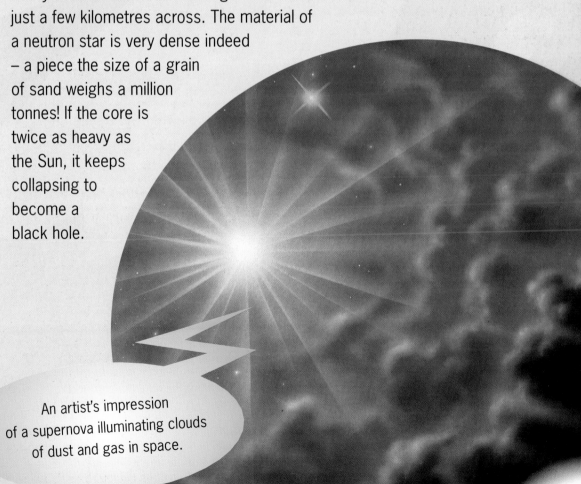

An artist's impression of a supernova illuminating clouds of dust and gas in space.

IS A BLACK HOLE REALLY A HOLE?

A black hole is not a solid object, like a planet such as the Earth, but it is shaped like a sphere. **Astronomers think that at the centre of a black hole there is a very strange object indeed – if you can call it an object. It is a single point in space with infinite density called a singularity. The mass is not infinite, but the density is, because the point has no size. Unfortunately, because nothing can escape from the black hole, we can't see whether this is true or not! If the singularity theory is correct, it means that when a massive star collapses, all the material in it disappears into the singularity. So there is not really a hole, or a tunnel to anywhere else in the Universe, inside a black hole.**

The event horizon

A black hole has no surface. You can think of it as beginning at the **gravitational radius**. The sphere at the gravitational radius is called the event horizon. The event horizon is the point of no return. Anything that crosses it can never come back. Outside the event horizon is a region called the ergosphere. Anything inside the ergosphere rotates with the black hole, but it has the possibility of escaping.

Dips and holes

Einstein imagined space as a sheet of rubber material which represents space and time, with dents in it created by the **gravity** of bodies. A planet makes a tiny dip in the surface and a star a much greater dip. You can imagine that things could escape from the dips, but never from the bottomless funnel created by a black hole.

An illustration of Einstein's idea of a black hole distorting space and time to form a bottomless funnel.

INTO A BLACK HOLE ...

It is a common belief (probably created by science-fiction films) that a black hole 'sucks' in everything around it with its massive **gravity**. This is not what happens. An object which passes by a black hole a long distance away will change direction because of the black hole's gravity but carry on its journey. Objects can **orbit** a black hole just as the Earth orbits the Sun, but their orbits are not circular. Only objects which pass very close to or aim straight for a black hole disappear into it.

Many misconceptions about what happens in black holes come from science-fiction films and TV programmes, such as Star Trek.

Gravitational tides

Before imagining what it would be like to fall into a black hole, we need to look once more at **gravitational fields**. The further you get from the centre of a body, the weaker the gravitational field is. For example, when you are standing on the Earth's surface, the field is stronger at your feet than at your head. This difference in strength is called a gravitational tide. It tries to stretch you with a **force** called tidal force. You don't notice it on Earth because it is extremely small. But on the edge of a black hole it is very much bigger.

Over the horizon

So what would happen if you flew your spacecraft towards a black hole? The first thing to say is that it would not be a wise move! The gravity of the black hole would accelerate your spacecraft to faster and faster speeds. By the time you reached the event horizon, you would be travelling at the speed of light. Once over it, you would cease to exist and become part of the hole's **singularity** within a millionth of a second.

But before reaching the event horizon, your spacecraft and your body would have been pulled apart by tidal forces of the massively strong gravitational field. Even the atoms of your body would be ripped apart. Nasty! Strangely, tidal forces get smaller the bigger the black hole is. So you would survive longer – but only until the event horizon.

Stranger still would be the experience of a person watching you going into the black hole. Einstein's laws say that time slows down in strong fields. But not for you, only as far as someone outside the field is concerned. This means that for a person watching you, you would take forever to reach the event horizon!

SEARCHING FOR BLACK HOLES

So far in this book, everything has been theory. This was all worked out before the middle of the 20th century and before anybody had even looked for a real black hole in space. In fact, it was not until the 1960s that **astronomers** began to search properly for black holes. Even then, many astronomers found it hard to accept that black holes really existed because the theory was so far removed from the world of astronomy they knew and understood. Some astronomers refused to discuss black holes. Others said that even if black holes did exist, they would be impossible to find.

The Hubble Space Telescope was launched in 1990. It orbits the Earth and can give us much better images of space than any telescope on Earth.

Spot the black hole

Black holes are not easy to find. For a start, they are black! No light or anything else comes out of them, making them completely invisible to a telescope. Secondly, in astronomical terms, they are very tiny indeed. For example, a black hole formed by the collapse of a giant star would have an event horizon perhaps just 30 kilometres across.

Thirdly, astronomers realized that if black holes were made from massive stars, then the nearest ones would be dozens of light years away (a light year is the distance light travels in a year – about 10 million million kilometres). Even the most powerful telescopes could not pick out an object so small at such a huge distance – it would be like spotting a grain of sand, 0.1 millimetres across, on the Moon from the Earth.

The only way to find a black hole is to look for evidence of its effect on the other bodies in the space around it. These effects should be quite large because of the immensely strong **gravity** around the black hole.

Binary stars

The first approach astronomers took was to look for black holes in binary star systems. A binary system is made up of two stars close together which **orbit** around each other. Most stars in the Universe are in binary systems. Astronomers realized that if they saw a single star moving as if it was in a binary system, then its companion could be a black hole. Astronomers in the former **USSR** and USA found many cases which could be black holes, but this was not proof; the other body could be another sort of dead star, such as a neutron star (see page 15).

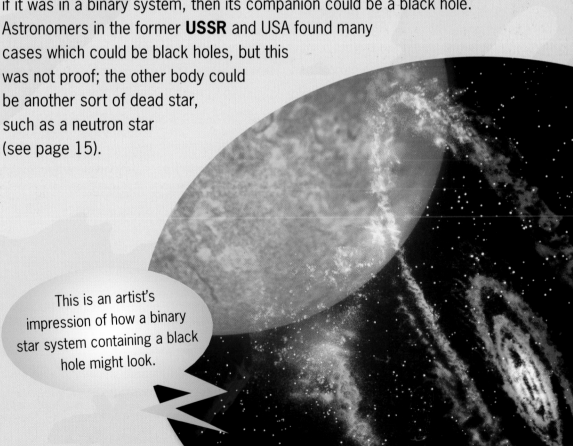

This is an artist's impression of how a binary star system containing a black hole might look.

X-RAY PROOF

After failing to find a definite black hole in a binary star, **astronomers** decided to look into gas **nebulae**. They realized that the gas and dust of a nebula could fall into a black hole and, if it did, would accelerate to such high speed that it would be heated to extremely high temperatures, giving out not just light, but other types of **electromagnetic radiation**, such as radio waves. Using radio telescopes, they scanned likely nebulae looking for radio waves coming from them. Unfortunately, this search proved fruitless too. It may have been that there were black holes where they were looking, but that the amount of gas and dust going in to them was so small that the radio waves were too weak to detect.

X-ray binaries

Astronomers did not give up. In 1966, they decided to look again at binary stars. They realized that if one of the pair of stars in a binary star was in fact a black hole, and if the other star and the black hole were close together, then the huge gravitational pull of the black hole would pull gas from the outer layers of the star into the hole.

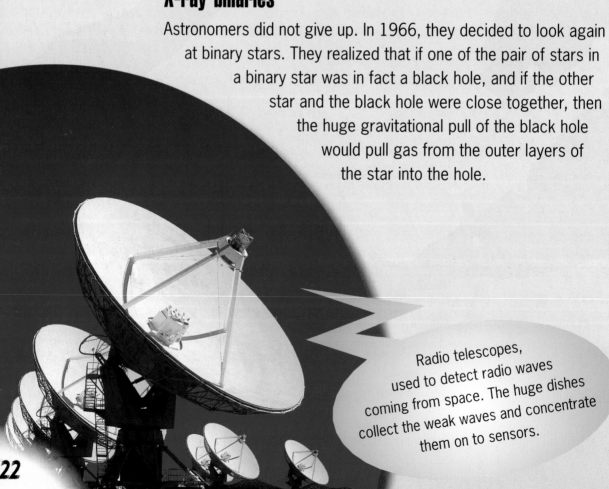

Radio telescopes, used to detect radio waves coming from space. The huge dishes collect the weak waves and concentrate them on to sensors.

The gas would spiral at enormous speed around the hole before falling in, creating immense heat and, more importantly, **X-rays**. But first they had to launch an X-ray telescope into space to detect the X-rays (see below).

There was one more problem. **Pulsars** create X-rays, too. An X-ray-producing binary star would either contain a pulsar or a black hole. But if they calculated from the motion of the binary stars that the dark one had a mass greater than twice that of the Sun, then it was probably a black hole rather than a pulsar.

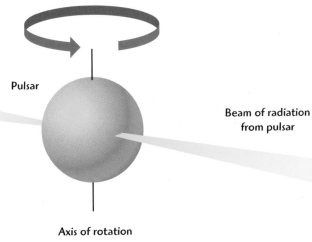

A pulsar acts like a lighthouse. It sends out two beams of radiation as it spins round.

Pulsar

Beam of radiation from pulsar

From Earth, we detect a pulse of radiation each time a beam sweeps by.

Axis of rotation

A pulsar is a spinning neutron star, sometimes formed after the collapse of a star at the end of its life.

X-ray astronomy

Unlike light, X-rays cannot penetrate the Earth's atmosphere. So X-rays from space cannot be detected from the Earth's surface. In order to look for them, it was necessary to launch a special telescope into **orbit** around the Earth. The first X-ray telescope, called UHURU, was launched from Kenya in 1970. It soon found the first X-ray binaries.

CASE STUDIES

Cygnus X-1

The first candidate for a black hole was found in 1971 in the **constellation** of Cygnus. The source of **X-rays** in the constellation is called Cygnus X-1, and is about 6,000 light years from Earth. At the source is a blue, super-giant star, 20 times more massive than our Sun. Every five and a half days it makes an **orbit** of its binary companion, which is invisible, but is ten times more massive than our Sun. Because it is a source of X-rays and so massive, **astronomers** believe it is a black hole, formed by a collapsed super-giant star.

Gas that is pulled from the super-giant star does not go straight into the black hole. Instead, it travels in a huge spiral and goes into orbit around the black hole. It forms a disc around the hole called an accretion disc. Friction between the layers of the disc makes the gas extremely hot, making it release huge amounts of energy. The friction also makes the inner layers gradually slow and fall into the hole.

Since Cygnus X-1 was discovered, several other black hole candidates have been found. Since most stars in our **galaxy** are in binary systems and millions of them are super-giants, it is likely that there are millions of black holes in our galaxy alone.

An artist's impression of the X-ray binary Cygnus X-1, showing gas from the star spinning into its black hole partner.

M87 galaxy

Dying stars might not be the only source of black holes. Many galaxies have extremely 'active' centres which give out strong X-rays and radio waves. The source of these waves could be a massive black hole, big enough to rip apart any stars that came within reach.

In 1994, the Hubble Space Telescope photographed the M87 galaxy. The images showed strong activity in its centre – far greater than normal star activity would account for. At its centre is thought to be a super-massive black hole as wide as our Solar System and with the mass of two billion Suns.

Measurements of the speed of gases in the centre of our own galaxy, the Milky Way, show that there is probably a massive black hole there too. In 2000, scientists revealed that every galaxy they had studied using the Hubble Space Telescope appeared to have a black hole at its centre. This told them that black holes may be essential in the formation of galaxies.

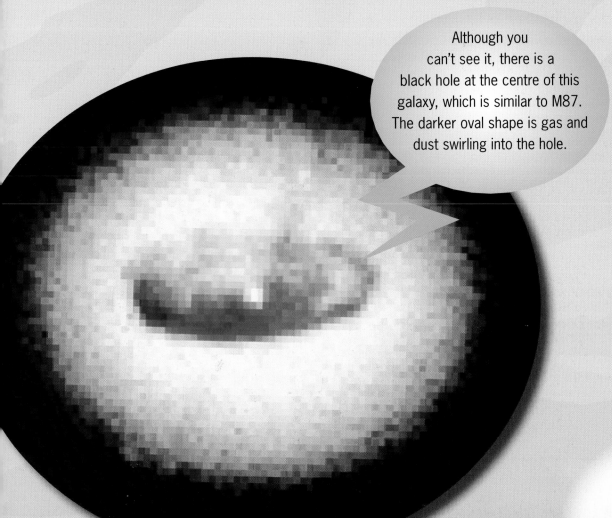

Although you can't see it, there is a black hole at the centre of this galaxy, which is similar to M87. The darker oval shape is gas and dust swirling into the hole.

NEW IDEAS

So far, you have seen how theory predicts that black holes are formed by the collapse of massive stars and are often at the centres of **galaxies**. The theory also says that nothing can escape from a black hole. This must also mean that black holes can never be destroyed. But can this be true? English physicist Stephen Hawking (b. 1942), who has come up with many new theories about the Universe, thinks it might not be.

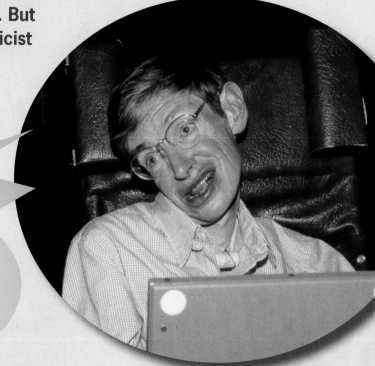

Professor Stephen Hawking continues his research into relativity and black holes despite having motor neurone disease, which affects his movement and speech.

Early black holes

Hawking suggests that many small black holes were formed during the **Big Bang**, when the Universe was born in an unimaginably enormous explosion. These could not have been formed by the collapse of stars because there were no stars then. These black holes would now be undetectable because all the matter around them, such as close-by stars and gas would have fallen in, and so **X-ray emissions** would have stopped.

Hawking also suggests that some of the black holes made in the early moments of the Universe were mini black holes, perhaps no larger than a house. These would gradually have dispersed all their energy and finally disappeared.

Worm holes

Another of Hawking's theories is even stranger than the theories we have looked at so far. Hawking thinks that the **singularity** theory for the centre of a black hole may not be correct. Instead of the singularity, there is a sort of hole called a worm hole which leads into another Universe, completely separate from our own.

Black holes and the Universe

The study of black holes could help **astronomers** to work out a great deal about how the Universe as a whole works, how it started in the first place and what might happen in the future. There may be similarities between what happens at the singularity in a black hole and what happened during the Big Bang.
In fact, the whole Universe may have been born from a super-massive black hole!

At the bright centre of this photograph is a quasar, a super-bright, distant galaxy which emits strong radio waves, perhaps because of a massive black hole at its centre.

WHAT DO YOU THINK?

The mystery surrounding black holes is strange in itself because the existence of black holes was predicted long before **astronomers** could find any real evidence for them. Now some evidence has been found. So far, it matches the theories, so it seems to prove that black holes do exist.

Are the theories about what happens in a black hole correct?

Sounds convincing...
- So far, black holes match the predictions of scientists working before black holes had actually been discovered

- The way stars and planets behave around a black hole supports the theories about what happens inside it

- Scientists are continuing to find out more and more about black holes.

But what about...?
- Just because some of the theories are proven to be true, doesn't mean that they're all true

- Some of the theories about changes to the passing of time and a singularity with no size but an **infinite mass** are just too weird to be true – aren't they?

- We can never travel to a black hole so we'll never really know if the theories are true.

The theories about what happens in black holes predict things we find hard to comprehend because they are so weird. But perhaps in many years time we will learn to accept them.

What about some of the other theories about black holes? Do you think any of them might be true? Look at the list of theories below and think about the pros and cons of each. Are they all correct?

- Time is different for objects travelling at the speed of light

- There are worm holes leading to a universe completely separate from our own

- Black holes are at the centre of every **galaxy**, including our own.

The evidence of these theories is often very difficult to understand but see what more you can find out about black holes.

What are your conclusions? Is the evidence for black holes strong enough to conclude that they definitely exist? Do you have any theories of your own? Try to keep an open mind. Remember that science is constantly evolving and new discoveries are being made all the time. Just because something can't be proved scientifically now, doesn't mean this will always be the case.

The bright spot at the bottom-right of this photograph is a supernova – an exploding star – which may leave another black hole in the Universe.

GLOSSARY

astronomer a person who studies space and the objects in space, such as stars, planets and moons

astrophysics the mathematics and physics that govern what happens in space. Astrophysicists also try to explain new discoveries in space.

Big Bang the unimaginably large explosion that most astrophysicists think happened when the Universe began. Before the Big Bang, space did not exist.

constellation a group of stars in the sky that seems to form a pattern. Constellations have names which were given to them by ancient peoples.

density the amount of matter contained in a certain space. Density is measured in kilograms per metre cubed.

diameter the distance from one side of a circle to the other, measured through the centre of the circle

electromagnetic radiation waves or rays given off by substances. There is a whole family of different types of electromagnetic radiation, including light, radio waves, X-rays, microwaves and infra-red rays.

emissions the electromagnetic radiation coming from an object

force a push or a pull

galaxy an enormous group of stars. The stars in space are contained in galaxies rather than being spread evenly through it. A typical galaxy contains hundreds of millions of stars.

geometry the study of the shape of objects and how the shapes can be written down mathematically

gravitational field the area around a body where other objects are affected by its gravity

gravitational radius the distance from the centre of a black hole to the event horizon. Anything inside the event horizon cannot escape from the black hole.

gravity the force that attracts (pulls) all objects towards all other objects, including you to the Earth

infinite never ending or too big to measure

infinity a point immeasurably far away in distance or time

nebula (plural nebulae) an enormous cloud of gas and dust in space

orbit the path that an object, such as a moon, follows around another object, such as a planet

pulsar a neutron star (the remains of a giant star) which rotates, sending out radio waves and X-rays

radius the distance from the centre to the outside of a circle. The radius is equal to half its diameter.

singularity the point at the centre of a black hole which has no size but is infinitely heavy

USSR the former Soviet Union, which has now divided into separate countries, including Russia and the Ukraine

vacuum a place where there is nothing, not even air. The regions between the stars and planets contain a vacuum.

X-ray a type of electromagnetic radiation which can pass through soft materials such as cloth but not through hard materials such as metals

Find out more

You can find out more about black holes in books and on the Internet. Use a search engine such as www.yahooligans.com to search for information. A search for the words "black hole" will bring back lots of results, but it may be difficult to find the information you want. Try refining your search to look for some of the people and ideas mentioned in this book, such as "Albert Einstein" or "Hubble Space Telescope".

More Books to Read

Black Holes and Other Space Oddities, Alex Barnett (Dorling Kindersley, 2002)

Stargazer's Guides: What's Inside a Black Hole?, Andrew Solway (Heinemann Library, 2006)

Websites

www.nasa.gov - official site of NASA. Includes loads of images from the Hubble Space Telescope (hubble.nasa.gov)

http://www.bbc.co.uk/science/space - a great reference site for everything to do with space

INDEX